A Rookie reader

Kate's Surprise

Written by Ann Burg
Illustrated by Phyllis Harris

Children's Press®
A Division of Scholastic Inc.
New York • Toronto • London • Auckland • Sydney
Mexico City • New Delhi • Hong Kong
Danbury, Connecticut

For Alexander Louis, who loves surprises.
—A. B.

For mom and dad.
Thanks for all your wonderful support through the years.
—P.H.

Reading Consultant

Cecilia Minden-Cupp, PhD
Former Director of the Language and Literacy Program
Harvard Graduate School of Education
Cambridge, Massachusetts

Cover design: The Design Lab
Interior design: Herman Adler

Library of Congress Cataloging-in-Publication Data

Burg, Ann E.
  Kate's surprise / by Ann Burg; illustrated by Phyllis Harris.
      p. cm. — (Rookie reader: silent letters)
   ISBN-13: 978-0-531-17549-1 (lib. bdg.)   978-0-531-17781-5 (pbk.)
   ISBN-10: 0-531-17549-9 (lib. bdg.)   0-531-17781-5 (pbk.)
  1. English language—Vowels—Juvenile literature. I. Harris, Phyllis,
1962– ill. II. Title. III. Series.
  PE1157.B87 2007
  428.1—dc22   2006024387

Huge white snowflakes fall.
Pete wants to go outside.

He wants to take his snow tube,
and slide, slide, slide.

But Pete's throat is sore.
His nose is red and stuffy.

His head is hot.
His bones are cold.
His face is pale and puffy.

9

Pete's sister Kate takes
his snow tube for a ride.

11

Down the snowy slope,
she glides, glides, glides.

Pete watches from the window.
He wants to go out, too.

15

Kate looks back and smiles and waves.
She knows just what to do.

Kate hurries back inside.
She takes off her boots and coat.

She has a big surprise for Pete
and his scratchy, red sore throat.

"Pete, close your eyes!
I made you a special treat."

A three-scoop snowman
that's good enough to eat!

"MMMMM . . ." says Pete.

27

"That tastes super great!"

29

"I feel better already.
Thanks, Kate!"

31

Word List (92 words)

(Words in **bold** have the silent *e* sound.)

a	fall	just	she	thanks
already	feel	**Kate**	sister	that
and	for	knows	**slide**	that's
are	from	looks	**slope**	the
back	**glides**	**made**	**smiles**	three
better	go	mmmmm	snow	throat
big	good	**nose**	**snowflakes**	to
bones	great	off	snowman	too
boots	has	out	snowy	treat
but	he	**outside**	sore	**tube**
close	head	**pale**	special	wants
coat	her	**Pete**	stuffy	watches
cold	his	**Pete's**	super	**waves**
do	hot	puffy	**surprise**	what
down	**huge**	red	**take**	**white**
eat	hurries	**ride**	**takes**	window
enough	**inside**	says	**tastes**	you
eyes	I	scoop		your
face	is	scratchy		

About the Author

Ann Burg grew up writing stories for her family and her friends. She wrote articles for newspapers and has always kept a journal. This is her seventh children's book but her drawers are stuffed with many more stories and poems. Ann lives in upstate New York with her husband, two children, one dog, and one very special bear.

About the Illustrator

Growing up in greater Kansas City, Phyllis loved playing in the snow and still does.